Questions AND Answers

EXPLORATION AND DISCOVERY

Philip Brooks

KINGFISHER
Kingfisher Publications Plc
New Penderel House
283–288 High Holborn
London WC1V 7HZ
www.kingfisherpub.com

Produced by Scintilla Editorial Ltd
33 Great Portland Street
London W1W 8QG
www.scintilla-editorial.co.uk

First published by Kingfisher Publications Plc in 2002
10 9 8 7 6 5 4 3 2 1

1TR/0402/TIMS/UNI/130MA

ISBN 0 7534 0710 8

Printed in China

Author: Philip Brooks
Editors: John Birdsall and Hannah Wilson
Designer: Joe Conneally
Artwork archivists: Wendy Allison and Steve Robinson
Production: Jo Blackmore

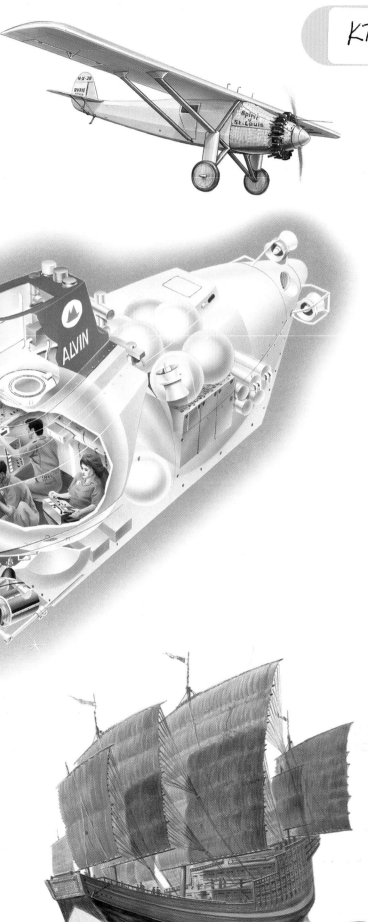

Contents

Ancient Empires

The people of the first great civilizations were remarkable travellers. The Greeks and Phoenicians set up far-flung trading colonies, the Egyptians went on an expedition to a mysterious land called Punt, while the Romans created the largest empire the world had ever seen. To achieve all this, they had to sail and march into unknown territory without maps, charts or even travellers' tales to tell them what they might find.

Where was the mysterious land of Punt?

In about 1500 BC, the Egyptian queen, Hatshepsut, sent five ships on a voyage to the land of Punt. They sailed down the Red Sea from where they probably turned south, so Punt was likely to have been somewhere in East Africa, on the Horn of Africa – possibly Somalia. The Egyptians brought back incense, spices, ivory, gold and leopard skins – all goods that could have come from this part of Africa.

How do we know about ancient voyagers?

There are few written records of the first explorers, but archaeologists have traced where they went by finding the items that they traded. Phoenicians (right), from the coast of Lebanon and Syria, sailed all around the Mediterranean between 1500 and 500 BC. They traded their famous glassware, pottery and dyed cloth all over the area, and their stout ships even reached Britain and West Africa.

How far did the Greeks travel?

As well as setting up colonies around the Mediterranean Sea, the Greeks sailed out into the Atlantic Ocean to trade and explore. Their most famous navigator, Pytheas, sailed around the British Isles in about 330 BC. He then travelled even farther north to a place he called Thule. No one knows for sure where Thule was – it may have been the coast of Norway, or even Iceland.

Why were the Phoenicians such great explorers?

The tall cedar trees that grew in the Phoenicians' homeland were ideal for building boats, and the Phoenicians soon became skilled ship-builders. Their strong vessels were powered by rows of oars and a single sail (above). These ships were very wide and, because they were so broad of beam, they could carry the large cargoes that were traded all around the Mediterranean.

Were the Romans great explorers?

As well as empire builders, the Romans were great explorers. They sailed the Mediterranean in their galleys, and crossed the North Sea to Britain. But they were more at home on land. As the Roman armies marched across mainland Europe, surveyors and cartographers followed close behind, mapping the conquered lands.

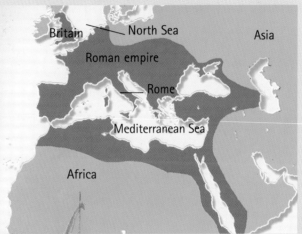

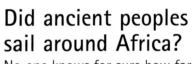

Britain — North Sea — Asia
Roman empire
— Rome
Mediterranean Sea
Africa

Did ancient peoples sail around Africa?

No one knows for sure how far south the Mediterranean explorers travelled. Hanno, a famous Phoenician sailor, followed the coast of West Africa. He explored the River Senegal and some of the coast beyond. The Egyptian expedition to Punt probably went far down Africa's eastern coast. The Greek historian, Herodotus (right), said that the Egyptians claimed to have sailed so far that the Sun rose on their right, but Herodotus did not believe them. Southern African sailors, who have left no records of their voyages, probably sailed farther and knew their coast better than these voyagers from the north.

Quick-fire Quiz

1. Which type of timber did the Phoenicians use for ship-building?
a) Oak
b) Ash
c) Cedar

2. Where might Thule have been?
a) Iceland
b) Egypt
c) East Africa

3. Which animal skins did the Egyptians bring back from Punt?
a) Elephant
b) Deer
c) Leopard

4. How did the Romans prefer to explore?
a) By boat
b) On foot
c) By air

The Mysterious East

The emperors of China ruled a huge part of eastern Asia, but were keen to find out more about the lands that lay beyond their control. Chinese explorers travelled huge distances, mostly overland, to what is now Mongolia, India and Central Asia. As a result of these journeys, they forged links between some of the greatest empires the world has ever known.

Why was religion important to early travellers?

Many early Chinese explorers were Buddhists (left). Buddhism began in India, and Chinese monks such as Fa Hsien wanted to find out more about their faith. In the fourth century AD, Fa Hsien travelled from China to India to study in Buddhist monasteries. His expedition took about 15 years and included a long trek through the deserts of northern China and the Hindu Kush mountain range, and a trip down India's River Ganges.

How did people travel in India?

Although the Chinese were used to horses, in India, they came across an awesome new form of transport – the elephant (right). Hsüan Tsang, a Buddhist traveller who went to India in the seventh century AD, reported how impressed he was by the elephant that he rode in the north of the country.

Who was Zheng He?

During the 15th century AD, Admiral Zheng He was ordered by the emperor of China to explore 'countries beyond the horizon'. Aboard the most advanced ship of its time (below), Zheng He sailed south to Indonesia and then west to India and Africa. Then, in 1433, China decided to halt all further exploration, so it burned its ocean-going ships. As a result, Europeans 'discovered' China, instead of China 'discovering' Europe.

Zheng He's flagship had nine masts and was 130 metres long

Why were Chinese emperors keen to explore Asia?

Chinese emperors often sent their representatives to explore the world around them on their behalf (above). In the second century BC, Emperor Wu Ti sent his official Chang Ch'ien to Central Asia, hoping to find allies who would help China in their wars against the Huns. The Huns discovered what Chang Ch'ien was trying to do, however, and captured him. Eventually he escaped, and was successful in forging alliances with some of the peoples of Central Asia.

Did explorers face many dangers?

Explorers often had to pass through dangerous enemy lands and some, such as Chang Ch'ien, risked being captured or killed. They also faced rough, mountainous country, bad weather and even attacks by wild animals. Not surprisingly, many of the explorers who set out were never seen or heard of again.

What treasures did the Chinese explorers collect?

Many of the early explorers went in search of gold and other riches, as well as the opportunity to trade. But the Buddhist explorers of China, such as Fa Hsien and Hsüan Tsang, also took home religious relics and holy books. Scrolls containing prayers and the works of the great Buddhist teachers, statues of the Buddha (right), and other religious objects, were eagerly collected and transported back to China.

In comparison, Columbus' flagship, the *Santa Maria*, had three masts and was 26 metres long

Quick-fire Quiz

1. How far west did Zheng He sail?
a) As far as Sri Lanka
b) As far as Arabia
c) As far as Africa

2. On which river in India did Fa Hsien travel?
a) The Indus
b) The Ganges
c) The Penneru

3. Which people imprisoned Chang Ch'ien?
a) The Huns
b) The Goths
c) The Romans

4. What was Hsüan Tsang's religion?
a) Buddhism
b) Christianity
c) Hinduism

Journeys of the Vikings

The Vikings, Norsemen from modern-day Norway, Denmark and Sweden, were the most famous travellers in Europe between the eighth and 11th centuries. In their elegant ships, they raided the coasts of northern Europe, striking fear into the locals. They voyaged into the North Atlantic to Iceland, Greenland and beyond.

Who was Erik the Red?

Erik the Red (above), a Viking from Iceland, was banished from his home for killing a man. Sailing westwards, in about 981, he discovered an icy waste. He named the place 'Greenland' to encourage other Vikings to settle there.

Which type of ships did the Vikings use?

For long voyages and trading expeditions, the Vikings used sturdy boats with square sails. About 12 metres in length and 3.3 metres across the beam, these boats had plenty of room for passengers or cargo. A few oars were carried for use when there was no wind.

Did Viking ships sail up rivers?

The Vikings built all kinds of boats, including some that they could row or sail up rivers. Some of their most famous voyages were along the rivers Volga and Dnieper, taking them to the Caspian and Black seas. They founded the settlements of Kiev and Novgorod, where the Vikings were called the 'Rus', perhaps the origin of the word 'Russian'.

Map labels: Greenland, Iceland, Norway, Sweden, Russia, British Isles, Mediterranean Sea, Caspian Sea, Black Sea, North America, Newfoundland, Atlantic Ocean, Africa, South America, Indian Ocean

Longship labels: Sail support, Carved figurehead, Steering oar, Square sail, Rowers' shields

Why did the Vikings travel such great distances?

The Vikings became infamous for their raids, but they travelled for other reasons too. Good farmland was scarce in their homeland (modern-day Scandinavia) so they sailed great distances in search of places where they could settle and grow crops. The Vikings also travelled in order to trade – Viking traders journeyed as far as Russia and the Mediterranean Sea.

What were longships?

Longships (above) were long, sleek vessels that the Vikings used for warfare and raiding. A typical longship was about 17.5 metres in length, but only 2.5 metres wide. Like a cargo ship, it had a square sail, but it also had a row of oar ports on each side. With 24 men rowing, these ships could mount rapid attacks and escape quickly.

Did the Vikings discover America?

Yes! In the year 1001, nearly 500 years before the time of Christopher Columbus, Leif Eriksson (above), the son of Erik the Red, was on a voyage to Greenland – but he took the wrong course. He finally struck land at a place he named Vinland. This was almost certainly Newfoundland, Canada, where the remains of a Viking settlement have been found at a place called L'Anse-aux-Meadows. Eriksson probably called the place Vinland ('vine-land') because he found berries there that he thought were grapes.

Quick-fire Quiz

1. Aside from raiding and trading, why did the Vikings go on long journeys?
a) To find new land for settlement
b) To visit their friends
c) To fight in wars

2. How were longships usually powered?
a) With oars
b) With sails
c) With both a sail and oars

3. Who was Leif's father?
a) Harold Bluetooth
b) Erik the Red
c) Thor

4. Where was Vinland?
a) Greenland
b) Iceland
c) Newfoundland

The Islamic World

By the 10th century, the Muslim empire stretched right across northern Africa, and north to Iran and Iraq. Many Muslims were notable traders, while others were scholars eager to find out more about the world. Some Muslims believed that it was vital to convert other peoples to the Islamic faith. For these three reasons – trade, scholarship and religion – exploration was a key part of the Muslim way of life.

Did the Muslims make maps?

The Muslims made maps in the 12th century that showed the land masses of the world. These maps were nowhere near as accurate as modern maps, but they were better than others available at the time. One scholar, Al Idrisi, wrote a guidebook for travellers as well as producing maps and a globe. The globe showed that the Muslims, unlike many other peoples of the time, knew that Earth was round.

What dangers did ancient explorers face on their journeys?

Journeying through unknown country brought with it many dangers. In North Africa, the explorer Ibn Battuta faced attacks by bandits and an unfamiliar and harsh climate – in the Atlas Mountains, he was even caught in a snowstorm. On his sea voyage to the Far East, he was attacked by pirates and nearly shipwrecked.

How did travellers cross the dry, sandy deserts of Africa and Arabia?

Local tribespeople and explorers usually crossed deserts by camel. Merchants would travel across the desert to visit towns such as Timbuktu and Takedda in large groups called 'caravans'. It was much safer to travel with a caravan than to venture out alone. A well-armed and provisioned group of travellers could defend itself if attacked by robbers. A caravan could also share food and water if delayed on its journey by sandstorms.

Which type of boats did Islamic sailors use?

In the Red Sea and Indian Ocean, Islamic sailors used the dhow, which had a sharp prow, a flat stern and triangular 'lateen' sails – ideal for the winds in coastal waters. Muslim pirates from North Africa used similarly rigged 'corsairs', which also had oars for rapid attack or getaway. When Ibn Battuta travelled farther east, he used the much-larger Chinese junks – ships with flat bottoms and square sails.

Corsair

Dhow

Chinese junk

Who was the greatest of the early Muslim travellers?

Ibn Battuta, a 14th-century explorer from Morocco in north-west Africa, was the greatest of the Muslim travellers. Ibn made long journeys across the Arabian peninsula, even longer trips across northern and western Africa, and a sea journey to India and China. His years of travelling taught him how to communicate with new peoples, and how to cross deserts – by travelling at night, when it was cool.

Ibn Battuta

The constellation Cepheus

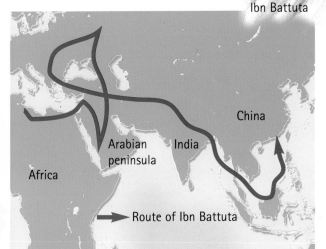

China

Arabian peninsula

India

Africa

→ Route of Ibn Battuta

How did Muslim scholars help their travellers?

Muslim scholars were skilled in many fields, including astronomy and geography. They built observatories and mapped the star constellations, often as human figures (above), and they worked out how to use the stars for navigation. Islamic scientists were also the first to make an instrument called the astrolabe. This device enabled explorers to measure the height of the Sun or a star, and so work out their position on Earth.

Quick-fire Quiz

1. Which shape did the Muslims believe Earth was?
   a) Round
   b) Flat
   c) Square

2. Which of these places was not visited by Ibn Battuta?
   a) North Africa
   b) Australia
   c) China

3. Why did Ibn Battuta travel in the desert at night?
   a) To navigate by the stars
   b) To avoid pirates
   c) Because it was cooler

4. Which shape are a dhow's sails?
   a) Square
   b) Triangular
   c) Rectangular

Across Asia

The trade route that connected China with the West was called the 'Silk Road' after the most valuable material that was carried along it. It was really a series of different roads across Central Asia, linking the major cities of China with Baghdad in Iraq. From Baghdad, the route continued westwards to the Mediterranean ports, where ships picked up goods and took them on to western Europe and North Africa.

Who was Marco Polo?

Marco Polo was an Italian merchant and traveller from Venice. He was born in the 13th century, when Venice was one of Europe's richest trading ports. His father and uncle, Niccolo and Maffeo Polo, were also notable explorers. Niccolo and Maffeo were two of the first Europeans to travel all the way along the Silk Road to China. Marco went with them on their second expedition.

Marco Polo

What was traded on the Silk Road?

Merchants carried many things other than silk along the Silk Road. Chinese traders took porcelain, jade and spices westwards as these were always sure to be snapped up by buyers in the West. All the goods were sold for large sums of money because the cost of transporting them such long distances was so high. Western merchants often sent horses and precious metals back to China.

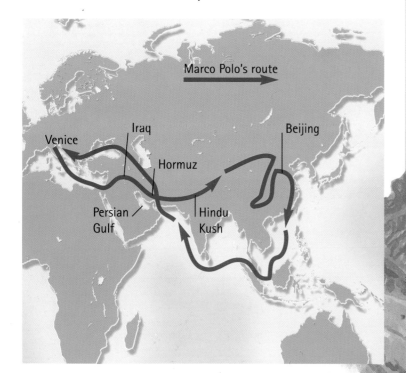

Marco Polo's route

Venice
Iraq
Hormuz
Beijing
Persian Gulf
Hindu Kush

Where did Marco Polo travel?

From Venice, Marco Polo journeyed through Iraq, and along the Persian Gulf, before setting out on a long land journey from Hormuz (above). He then travelled northwards before turning east and crossing Afghanistan (right), the Hindu Kush mountain range and the Gobi Desert. More than three years later, he arrived at the emperor of China's summer palace at Shangdu, before finally travelling south to the winter palace at Cambaluc (modern-day Beijing).

Why was silk so valuable?

Only the Chinese knew how to make silk, and they guarded the secret carefully. As silk was so rare, they could charge a high price for it. The price was forced up further as the cloth passed from merchant to merchant along the Silk Road – each trader had to make a profit. The costs of transport and the taxes charged by the Chinese emperor also added to the cost. Although silk was expensive, rich people in European cities such as Florence (above right) loved the luxury of silk clothes and were prepared to pay for it.

Quick-fire Quiz

1. Why was silk so rare?
 a) It came only from Florence
 b) Only the Chinese knew how to make it
 c) It was expensive

2. Where was Marco Polo's home?
 a) Venice
 b) Verona
 c) Versailles

3. What did Kublai Khan give to Niccolo and Maffeo Polo?
 a) A cup of tea
 b) An armed escort
 c) Special gold 'passports'

4. Which three things were often carried on the Silk Road?
 a) Timber, cotton and iron
 b) Shoes, socks and slippers
 c) Porcelain, jade and spices

How did the Polos travel so freely?

In the Middle Ages, it was not always easy to travel across foreign lands. On their first visit to Asia, Niccolo and Maffeo were given special 'passports' by Kublai Khan, the Chinese emperor (left). These were tablets of gold engraved with instructions ordering officials to allow the Polos to pass safely along their route. They were also helped on their way by donkeys, horses and camels.

How do we know about Marco Polo's adventures?

After Marco Polo returned to Europe, a book was published about what he had seen. Some of the things described in

the book, such as people with the head and tail of a dog, were clearly imagined! But his descriptions of the desert landscape, the mountains and the straight, bustling streets of Chinese cities (above) are probably based on what he saw.

The African Coastline

During the 15th century, Europeans began to explore the coast of western Africa. Sailing southwards into uncharted waters, they founded many trading colonies before venturing into the Indian Ocean and eventually reaching India. Most of these sailors were Portuguese. As well as making their country richer, they vastly increased their knowledge of Africa – a continent almost unexplored before this time.

Backstaff

Which navigational instruments did ships carry?

The ships carried compasses, but because of the differences between magnetic North and true North, experienced sailors relied on the Pole Star and the Sun to work out the direction of true North. The backstaff (above) and astrolabe (right) helped the navigator measure the height of the Sun or a star to determine the ship's latitude, or distance from the equator.

Astrolabe

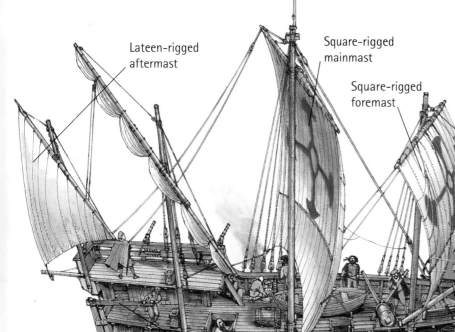

Lateen-rigged aftermast

Square-rigged mainmast

Square-rigged foremast

Stern rudder

Below-deck tiller

Which type of ships did they use?

The favourite ship of 15th-century explorers was the caravel (above). A caravel was quite a small and light ship, but one that had a broad beam so that it could carry plenty of stores in the hold. Caravels often carried two sets of sails – triangular 'lateen' sails, which were good for sailing in side winds or when the wind was light, and square sails that were ideal for sailing at speed with the wind behind.

Why were the Portuguese such notable explorers?

Portugal has a long coastline and so has produced many seafarers. But one man inspired Portugal's sailors to travel farther. Prince Henry (1394–1460) (right), the 'Navigator', founded an observatory and a school of navigation and paid for many voyages along the African coast. After Henry died, future kings of Portugal continued to fund expeditions.

Did they have maps of Africa?

Initially, Europeans only had maps of the north coast of Africa. Gradually, Portuguese navigators made new charts, showing the African coast more accurately and in more detail.
By the 1480s, they had mapped the west coast all the way south to the Cape of Good Hope.

Africa

Atlantic Ocean

Indian Ocean

Cape of Good Hope

Who first sailed around the Cape of Good Hope?

Bartolomeu Dias was the first explorer to round the Cape of Good Hope. When he reached the Cape in 1488, Dias wanted to sail on to India, but his men were fearful and exhausted, and the sea was stormy. So Dias only went a short way into the Indian Ocean before turning around and heading home.

Bartolomeu Dias

Which Portuguese explorer first reached India by sea?

After a long and stormy sea voyage (left), in 1498, Vasco da Gama became the first Portuguese explorer to reach India. Like Dias, he had hoped to trade with India, but Muslim merchants had got there first and they tried to keep the Portuguese out. Da Gama made another voyage in 1502. He founded colonies along the African coast and fought with the Muslims who had been attacking Portuguese merchants.

Quick-fire Quiz

1. What did Henry the Navigator found?
a) A school of navigation and an observatory
b) A port
c) A school for merchants

2. How did experienced sailors prefer to navigate?
a) By using a compass
b) By looking at the sky
c) By asking their shipmates

3. Which sails were best for sailing in light winds?
a) Square sails
b) Lateen sails
c) Topsails

4. Why didn't Vasco da Gama trade with India on his first voyage?
a) He did not reach India
b) The Indians had no money
c) Muslim merchants were already there

Atlantic Crossings

Christopher Columbus

In 1492, a navigator from Italy, Christopher Columbus (right), set off on a historic voyage. By crossing the Atlantic Ocean, Columbus became the first European since the Vikings to reach America. He returned laden with riches, and was soon followed by other Europeans eager to trade, plunder and set up colonies.

Why did Columbus want to cross the Atlantic?

The traders of Europe wanted to find the easiest route to Asia, where they could obtain valuable spices and other exotic goods that they could sell for a profit back home. The Portuguese were looking for a route to Asia via the African coast. Columbus, however, decided that, because the world was round, he could reach Asia if he sailed westwards across the Atlantic. He did not know that the Americas stood in his way (below left).

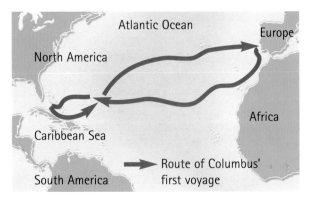

Atlantic Ocean

Europe

North America

Caribbean Sea

Africa

South America

→ Route of Columbus' first voyage

Where did Columbus drop anchor?

Columbus thought at first that he had landed in Asia, but in fact, he had only reached islands in the Caribbean Sea (above left). Here, he explored the Bahamas, then headed for the coast of the island Cuba. Finally, he dropped anchor on Haiti, whose warm climate and beautiful scenery greatly impressed him. As a tribute to King Ferdinand and Queen Isabella of Spain, who had financed his expedition, Columbus named the island 'Española', after 'España', the Spanish for 'Spain'.

What did Columbus discover in Haiti?

Columbus was frustrated when he first arrived in the Caribbean as he could not find the trading cities of the East. But the people of Haiti traded gold for his goods, and soon Columbus had sufficient wealth to repay his Spanish patrons.

What unusual things did Columbus bring back from the Caribbean?

On his voyages, Columbus gathered foods such as pineapples, sweetcorn and sweet potatoes, which had never been seen in Europe. The local people also gave him exotic birds such as parrots. Columbus and his men noticed that the islands of the Caribbean contained many other valuable resources from timber to herbs and spices.

Square main sail

Mizzen mast with lateen sail

Captain's cabin

Hold containing stores and trade goods

Caravel-style hull

Was Columbus a good navigator?

Although Columbus failed to reach Asia, he was a good navigator. He made three further voyages to the Caribbean, making important discoveries each time. On his third voyage, he sailed along the coast of Trinidad, and on his fourth, he navigated for hundreds of kilometres along the coast of Central America.

Which type of ship did Columbus sail?

On his first voyage, Columbus used three small, solidly built ships – the *Santa Maria* (above), the *Niña* and the *Pinta*. These ships had large, square sails that provided plenty of power at sea. But their small, caravel-style hulls made it a tight fit for the crews, which were about 40 in number – they often had to bed down among the stores on deck or in the ship's hold. Columbus originally sailed aboard the largest of his three ships, the *Santa Maria*, but after she was wrecked in the Caribbean, he transferred to the smaller *Niña* for the storm-racked return journey across the Atlantic.

The Longest Journey

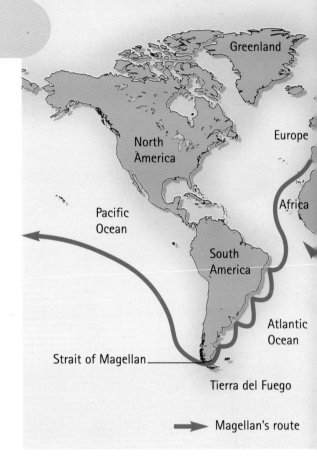

Before the 16th century, no one had ever sailed all the way around the world. Then, the Portuguese navigator Ferdinand Magellan and the British sailor Francis Drake both launched expeditions that achieved this remarkable feat. Their motive was not fame, however, but the fortune to be gained from finding a better trade route to the East.

Who was the first to sail all the way around the world?

When Ferdinand Magellan left Portugal in 1519 with five ships and 260 men, he had no idea of the historic importance of his voyage. This was because Magellan did not originally intend to sail around the world. And, as fate would have it, Magellan himself only travelled as far as the Philippines. But one of his ships with a crew of 18 men and captained by Sebastián de Elcano, carried on without him, completing the journey in 1522.

Why did Magellan fail to complete his journey?

Early in April 1521, Magellan reached Cebu in the Philippines. The ruler of this island was friendly. He converted to Christianity and gave Magellan gifts for the king of Spain, who was funding the expedition. But the king of nearby Mactan would not pay tribute, so Magellan fought him and his islanders. Magellan was killed by local warriors on Mactan on April 27, 1521.

How did the Pacific Ocean get its name?

During his epic voyage, Magellan and his men spent a bitterly cold and stormy winter in the South Atlantic Ocean. Icy waters lashed the ships, and icicles hung from the rigging (left). Then Magellan sailed through the narrow seaway between the southern tip of South America and the island of Tierra del Fuego – a channel now called the Strait of Magellan. After this, he came across a new area of water that was much quieter and calmer. Magellan named this new ocean the 'Pacific', which means 'peaceful'.

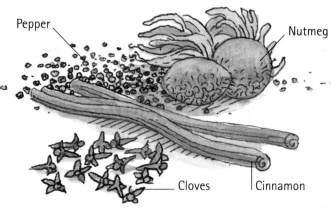

Pepper

Nutmeg

Cloves Cinnamon

What were the Spice Islands?

The Spice Islands was the old name for Maluku or the Moluccas, the group of islands lying roughly midway between the Philippines and Australia (left). In the 16th century, the people of these wooded, mountainous islands grew spices such as cloves, cinnamon and nutmeg (above) – all of which fetched high prices in the West.

Russia

Asia

Philippines

India

Australia

Indian Ocean

Philippines

Spice Islands

Australia

What was a privateer?

A privateer was a sailor who was given permission by his ruler to act as a pirate, raiding any ships he met and bringing the spoils back home. The most famous British privateer was Francis Drake (right), who sailed on behalf of Queen Elizabeth I. Drake began a round-the-world voyage in 1577, arriving back home in 1580. He sailed across the Atlantic, around South America, across the Pacific and Indian oceans, and back through the Atlantic. It is likely that his main goal was to plunder Spanish treasure ships.

Quick-fire Quiz

1. Who led Magellan's expedition after he died?
a) Sebastián de Elcano
b) Francis Drake
c) Vasco da Gama

2. What is the name of the seaway between South America and Tierra del Fuego?
a) The Pacific Strait
b) The Dardanelles
c) The Strait of Magellan

3. Where did Magellan die?
a) Spain
b) Mactan
c) Cebu

4. Which spices grew on the Spice Islands?
a) Cloves, cinnamon and nutmeg
b) Sandalwood, allspice and cumin
c) Tumeric, cardamon seeds and ginger

The South Seas

Europeans had long been fascinated by tales of the South Seas – the seas south of the equator – and their sun-drenched, paradise islands. In 1768, Englishman James Cook set sail to explore and chart this area thoroughly. During three great voyages, he mapped eastern Australia, sailed around New Zealand and was first to sail along the icy shores of Antarctica.

What dangers did the South Seas hold?

Voyages to the southern Pacific were so long that the crew often became ill, or suffered from a poor diet. But when the ships dropped anchor to take on fresh supplies, the sailors were sometimes attacked by locals. And, in uncharted waters, reefs were always a threat – Cook's ship, the *Endeavour*, was once stuck on Australia's Great Barrier Reef and needed repair (right). Icebergs were also a danger to those who, like Cook, sailed far to the south.

Why did Cook give his men limes to eat?

Most sailors in the 18th century suffered ill-health because of the bad conditions and lack of fresh food on long voyages. A common problem was scurvy – a disease that caused bleeding under the skin. Cook realized that his men became ill less often when they had a healthy diet. In particular, he noticed that if his crew ate limes (left), they hardly ever suffered from scurvy.

Why did Cook go to the Pacific?

Cook went to the South Pacific with several aims. On his first voyage, he went to the island of Tahiti (left) to observe the planet Venus pass in front of the Sun – an astronomical event best observed from this island. Cook also went in search of the legendary 'southern continent', and when he found New Zealand and Australia, he prove that they were separate islands. Later, he sailed to Antarctica to chart its virtually unknown waters and to record its wildlife.

What was Cook's ship like?

Cook's ship, the *Endeavour* (below), had humble origins as it was designed to carry coal around the coasts of Britain. But the vessel was tough and had plenty of room for more than 90 people, their supplies and the scientific specimens they collected on their voyage. And because Cook had sailed on similar vessels as a young man, he knew exactly how it behaved at sea.

Quick-fire Quiz

1. Which disease did limes help prevent?
a) Scabies
b) Rabies
c) Scurvy

2. Where did Cook go to observe the planet Venus?
a) Hawaii
b) Tahiti
c) Australia

3. Who was the first European to reach Australia?
a) Captain Cook
b) Dirk Hartog
c) Abel Tasman

4. What was Cook's ship originally used for?
a) Transporting slaves
b) Transporting coal
c) Exploration

How did Cook get on with the local people he met on his voyages?

Cook usually got on well with the people he came across. He traded with local people to get fresh food, and often won their trust. But he did encounter a few problems. On his first voyage, he had a skirmish with the Maoris on New Zealand's North Island (right). And on his final voyage, he got into a fight with people on Hawaii who stole one of his boats. Cook was stabbed to death in the fighting.

Who first sailed the South Seas?

Several Europeans sailed the South Seas before Cook. In 1616, Dutch sailor Dirk Hartog reached the west coast of Australia when he sailed too far east on a voyage to Java, Indonesia. In the 1640s, another Dutchman, Abel Tasman, discovered Tasmania and sighted New Zealand. In the late 17th century, British privateer William Dampier found the north-west coast of Australia.

Northern Passages

By the late 15th century, explorers from Europe realized that they might be able to reach Asia more quickly by using a northern route. Some tried sailing through the islands and ice floes of northern Canada. Others searched for a route north of Siberia. These seas were so cold and dangerous that many sailors perished, and it took hundreds of years before a ship finally made it through either route.

Why did so many seek a northern passage?

The search for a northern passage was driven by traders who wanted to find the quickest way to the spices and other riches of Asia. For Europeans, the voyage around the African coastline took too long. Some traders also hoped to find further sources of wealth along a northern route. In 1576, English sailor Martin Frobisher discovered 'gold' near the coast of Canada. Sadly, it turned out to be iron pyrites, or 'fool's gold' (above).

What happened when a ship got stuck in the ice?

When the Arctic Ocean froze in winter, vessels were often trapped by the growing mass of ice (left). Sometimes a ship would remain stuck until the spring thaw, by which time those on board might have run out of food or fuel. But the pressure of the ice was often so great that the timbers of wooden ships would be crushed, sending the crew to a cold and watery grave.

Are the northern passages used today?

Modern ships called icebreakers (above) regularly carry cargo through the North-east Passage from the Pacific to the Atlantic. Icebreakers have hulls reinforced with stainless steel. They pump high-pressure air into the water to break up the ice as they move. Some also have propellers on the front to help them smash their way through the ice.

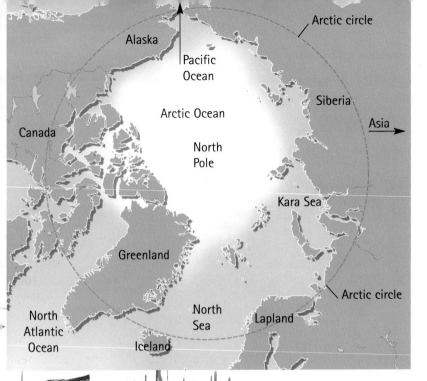

Where was the North-east Passage?

Navigators from Holland and Scandinavia tried to find a North-east Passage to the Pacific by sailing into the Arctic Ocean from the North Sea. Dutchman Willem Barents was one of the first to look for this route, in the late 16th century. Even when the weather was mild, however, he made it only to the Kara Sea, about halfway to the Pacific. Other Dutch explorers also tried to find a way through, but none were successful.

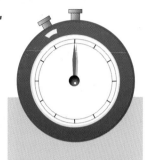

Where was the North-west Passage?

The North-west Passage was the route to Asia through the waters north of Canada (above left). Several British explorers tried to find this route. Henry Hudson died in 1611 on these frozen seas and, in 1845, Sir John Franklin, another British explorer, also perished looking for the North-west Passage.

Who first sailed the North-east Passage?

Finnish scientist and explorer Nils Nordenskjöld was the first to sail through the North-east Passage. He set out during the summer of 1878 in a strengthened whaling ship called the *Vega*. He almost made it to the Pacific before the winter, but was frozen in the ice and had to wait until the spring of 1879 to complete his journey.

Who finally sailed the North-west Passage?

Norwegian explorer Roald Amundsen (right) was the first to navigate through the North-west Passage, during a three-year expedition from 1903 to 1906. Amundsen, one of the greatest of all explorers, used a reinforced fishing boat and took on enough stores for a five-year voyage. His long stay in the frozen north taught him much about how to survive in icy conditions – knowledge he would put to use later when he journeyed to the South Pole.

Exploring North America

From the icy wastes of Canada to the tropical countries of Central America, North America covers a huge area and has been explored by many different people. Some came in peace or in the hope of making their fortune through trade. Others wanted to plunder what they could find and return with their riches to Europe. In each case, the explorers helped open up North America for all those who followed.

Why did Jefferson want Louisiana explored?

When French explorer Robert de La Salle first explored the Mississippi River in the 18th century, he claimed the region for France and named it Louisiana. More than 100 years later, the USA bought Louisiana from the French. President Thomas Jefferson (above centre) wanted the region explored, hoping that its large rivers would open up the West to trade.

Who were Lewis and Clark?

Meriwether Lewis was an infantry captain, and Clark was a retired lieutenant when they were commissioned by the president of the USA to explore the Missouri River and its tributaries (above). Both men were extremely able – Lewis was a good leader, and Clark was a skilled riverman and expert map-maker. They set out from St Louis in May 1804, crossed the Rocky Mountains and reached the Pacific at the mouth of the Columbia River in September 1806.

How did the explorers communicate with the native people they met?

Lewis and Clark made peaceful contact with a number of Native American tribes such as the Shoshone, Mandan, Sioux and Omaha. They were helped by Sacagawea, the Shonshone wife of one of the expedition members, who acted as an interpreter and a guide (right). The explorers learned from the native peoples how to build and handle canoes, which helped them to navigate fast-flowing rivers such as the Missouri. They also met chiefs who were willing to trade local produce for guns and other manufactured goods.

Who explored the Mississippi?

In 1672, Jacques Marquette, a French Jesuit missionary and explorer, and Louis Jolliet, a trader, set out to explore the Mississippi. They reached the point where it joins the Missouri the following year.

Marquette was not only a keen geographer, he was also interested in Native American language and culture, including customs such as the use of a special pipe (right), which indicated that he came in peace.

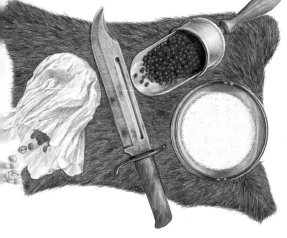

How did trade encourage exploration?

Canada was explored by Frenchmen Jacques Cartier, who arrived in 1535, and Samuel de Champlain, who explored the region from 1615-16. Once De Champlain had built up a profitable fur trade, French trappers began going deeper into the interior, exploring the rivers and founding trading posts where furs were traded for provisions (left).

Who explored Florida?

Florida was explored by Spaniard Hernando de Soto in 1539. In his search for cities of gold, De Soto killed and tortured thousands of Native Americans. His murderous trail led through Georgia, Carolina and Tennessee, until eventually he died beside the Mississippi having found none of the riches he sought.

Did the Spanish ever find El Dorado?

Although El Dorado, the city of gold, was just a legend, when Spanish nobleman Hernan Cortés (right) led an expedition to Mexico in 1519, he did find that the Aztec people had plenty of gold. Although he began dealing with the Aztecs peacefully, this did not last. Soon the Spanish were ruling Mexico, and ships laden with gold were heading back to Spain.

Quick-fire Quiz

1. By which river did De Soto die?
a) The Missouri
b) The Mississippi
c) The Amazon

2. Which people did Cortés' men fight?
a) The Sioux
b) The Aztecs
c) The Incas

3. Which tribe did Lewis and Clark encounter?
a) The Apache
b) The Sioux
c) The Cherokee

4. Which territory did the USA buy from the French?
a) Florida
b) Canada
c) Louisiana

Into Africa

For Europeans, Africa was once the 'Dark Continent', a frighteningly huge and largely unexplored region. But in the 19th century, a new-found curiosity about Africa began to grow. Funds were raised, and European adventurers set out to meet and study its peoples, map its deserts, mountains and jungles, and follow its many great rivers to their source.

What did explorers do at rapids and waterfalls?

Waterfalls and rapids were common along Africa's rivers, and explorers often had to carry their boats around them. This meant that they couldn't travel in large boats or carry too much equipment. American adventurer Henry Morton Stanley came up with a solution. His boat, the *Lady Alice*, was quite large, but made in sections that could be taken apart, allowing it to be carried with ease.

Why did Europeans first go to Africa?

Europeans first went to Africa to find slaves. Traders grew rich buying and selling Africans to people in the Caribbean and North America, and they did not explore much of Africa beyond the coast. Then, in 1788, Joseph Banks, a botanist who had travelled to the South Seas with James Cook, founded the African Association with the aim of discovering more about the continent – serious scientific exploration had begun at last.

How did explorers travel in Africa?

Explorers had to select the best means of transport for the local conditions. They used camels in the desert (right) and horses on the plains. In the forests and jungles, it was often best to travel along the rivers by boat. Many Europeans were fascinated by the Nile, and Richard Burton, John Hanning Speke and David Livingstone all searched for its source.

Why did Livingstone disappear?

David Livingstone was a Scottish doctor who went to Africa as a missionary to convert people to Christianity and care for the sick. But he became fascinated by the continent and went on several expeditions across southern Africa and along the Zambezi and Congo rivers. On an expedition to look for the source of the Nile, he ran into problems near Lake Tanganyika (below). His supplies ran out, his porters deserted him, and he became ill. All he could do was stay put, but no one knew where he was.

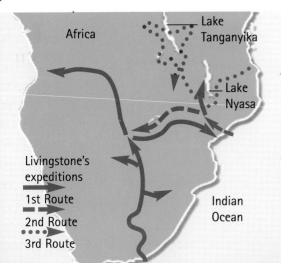

Africa

Lake Tanganyika

Lake Nyasa

Livingstone's expeditions

1st Route

2nd Route

3rd Route

Indian Ocean

Who sent Stanley to find Livingstone?

Henry Morton Stanley was a journalist employed by an American newspaper to find Dr Livingstone. Stanley took about 200 porters with him and arrived at Ujiji, near Lake Tanganyika, in late 1871. He finally greeted the missing explorer with the famous phrase, 'Dr Livingstone, I presume?' (above).

Who crossed the Sahara Desert?

One of the first European explorers to cross the Sahara Desert was Frenchman René Caillé. He reached Timbuktu in 1828, after a south-to-north crossing of the desert. Heinrich Barth, a German working for the British government, also travelled in the Sahara, in the 1850s. Barth, a true explorer, took time to get to know the country and its people, and to record what he saw.

Amazon and Andes

South America was irresistibly attractive to two very different kinds of explorer. Some were drawn by the prospect of conquest and limitless wealth. But others, especially naturalists in the 19th century, were fascinated by the region's dramatic scenery, variety of habitats and by species that no European had ever seen before.

Pizarro

Why did the Spanish journey to South America?

From their bases in the Caribbean and Panama, the Spanish heard rumours of fabulously rich civilizations in Mexico and South America. In 1531, Spanish leader Francisco Pizarro (above) set out with about 200 men to conquer the Inca people, whose empire stretched along the west coast of Peru. Using treachery to capture and murder the Inca emperor, Atahualpa (left), Pizarro quickly conquered Peru. He then forced the Incas to work as slaves in their silver and gold mines and shipped tonnes of gold objects back to Spain.

Which naturalists first explored the Andes?

In 1799, German scientist Alexander von Humboldt and Frenchman Aimé Bonpland (above) set out on a long journey through the Andes, a huge mountain range along the west coast of South America. Bonpland, a botanist, drew and collected many plants, some of which turned out to be useful medicines. Von Humboldt wrote about their travels in a huge 23-volume work.

Who were the Incas?

During the 16th century, the Incas controlled much of South America from southern Columbia to Chile. The Incas were highly sophisticated and they built roads, terraced farmlands and marvellous cities in the inhospitable mountains. The Inca emperor (right) was believed to be descended from the Sun god, who was worshipped in rituals and ceremonies.

Which ship made the first proper survey of South America's coastline?

During the 1830s, the British naval ship *HMS Beagle* sailed around virtually the entire coastline of South America. Its crew charted the coastal waters, while the naturalist on board collected and recorded wildlife from the mainland and the Falkland and Galapagos islands.

Why is the *Beagle's* expedition so famous?

The naturalist on the *Beagle* was a young man called Charles Darwin, who later became one of the best-known scientists of all time (above). Darwin carefully recorded all the plants and animals that were unknown in Europe. He used these observations when he wrote his most famous book, *On the Origin of Species*. This book gives the first explanation of evolution – the way in which the characteristics of living things change over time.

What dangers did Darwin face?

Darwin and the crew of the *Beagle* faced all the usual ocean perils when they sailed in the stormy waters of the South Atlantic. And Darwin's work as a naturalist brought fresh dangers. On one expedition in the Andes, he found himself dangerously near an active volcano (above). And on the island of Chiloé, he experienced an earthquake.

Why was the Amazon River attractive to explorers and naturalists?

Like the Nile in North Africa, the mighty Amazon River held an irresistible attraction for many explorers and naturalists. Englishmen Alfred Russel Wallace and Henry Walter Bates explored it in the mid-19th century. Keen scientists, they were fascinated by the rich variety of the wildlife. The Amazon rainforest was home to thousands of species unknown to science, from plants and insects to spectacular birds and mammals. Some of the birds, such as toucans (right), with their bright feathers and enormous bills, were among the most colourful and unusual that had ever been seen.

Quick-fire Quiz

I. Why were some of Bonpland's plants so useful?
a) They were unknown to science
b) They could be eaten by explorers
c) They could be used to make medicines

2. What theory did Darwin explain in his famous book?
a) The theory of exploration
b) The theory of evolution
c) The theory of revolution

3. What happened to Darwin on the island of Chiloé?
a) He experienced an earthquake
b) He saw an active volcano
c) He lost some of his specimens

4. Which people did Pizarro conquer?
a) The Maya
b) The Aztecs
c) The Incas

Crossing Australia

Soon after James Cook charted Australia's eastern coast, the first European settlers began to arrive. They understood that their new home was a vast island continent, but knew little more. To begin with, the settlers were fully occupied trying to make a living in the harsh environment. But by the mid-19th century, some of the more adventurous ones began to wonder what the heart of Australia was really like.

How did Australian exploration begin?
The first European settlers lived and farmed on the Australian coast. As they became successful, they began to look inland for more good sheep country (above). One of these early explorers was Edward John Eyre. During the mid-19th century, he explored much of South Australia and was the first man to cross southern Australia from Adelaide to Albany.

What began the race to cross Australia?
In 1859, the pace of exploration picked up when the government of South Australia offered a prize for the first person to complete a south-to-north crossing of the country. Until then, most explorers had only charted the rivers (left) and mapped coastal areas, and it was still believed that there might be a vast inland sea. Only the Aborigines really knew what lay at the heart of Australia.

Which European found Ayers Rock first?
In 1873, William Christie Gosse set out from Alice Springs to find an overland route to Perth in western Australia. Although Gosse had to turn back, he discovered a huge, 350-metre-high sandstone monolith. He named it 'Ayers Rock' after the head of South Australia's government, Sir Henry Ayers. The rock is now known by its Aboriginal name 'Uluru'.

Who were the first to cross Australia?

Burke, Wills, Gray and King set out from Melbourne in August 1860, taking with them 28 horses, 24 camels, 80 pairs of shoes and enough food for two years (left). They finally reached the Gulf of Carpentaria in early February (below). But despite being so well-equipped, a number of bad decisions, combined with the harsh climate, hindered their progress home. Gray died first, and then after reaching Cooper's Creek, Burke and Wills also died. King was found by local Aborigines and was the only one of the party to survive.

Gulf of Carpentaria

AUSTRALIA

Cooper's Creek

Broken Hill

Melbourne

Did the early explorers take Aboriginal guides?

Some of the early explorers took local guides with them. When Eyre crossed the Nullarbor Plain between Adelaide and Albany in 1840, he took his Aboriginal friend Wylie with him. He realized that local people regularly went on long journeys through the bush, often to visit sacred sites (right). They knew the country well and could find sources of food and water in the driest and barest of landscapes.

Quick-fire Quiz

1. What is the name of the plain between Adelaide and Albany?
a) Nullarbor Plain
b) Central Plain
c) Flinders Plain

2. Who was the first person to explore much of South Australia?
a) Robert Burke
b) Edward John Eyre
c) James Cook

3. Which forms of transport were used by Burke and Wills?
a) Camels and horses
b) Boats and rafts
c) Camels and elephants

4. What is Uluru made of?
a) Limestone
b) Granite
c) Sandstone

The World's Coldest Places

The North and South Poles and the world's highest mountains are the coldest places on Earth. For thousands of years, no one visited these ferociously inhospitable regions. By the late 19th century, however, intrepid explorers began to plan their conquest of these places, wanting to set foot where no humans had been before.

Who were the first to climb Everest?

In 1953, New Zealander Edmund Hillary and Tenzing Norgay, one of the Sherpa people from the slopes of the Himalayas in Nepal, were the first to the top of the world's highest mountain (below). All previous attempts to scale Everest's 8,848-metre peak had failed because of the snow and cutting winds, as well as the thin air, which makes breathing very difficult.

Why was it so difficult to cross the Arctic Ocean?

The Arctic Ocean is frozen all the time, and many cross the ice on sledges pulled by dog teams (above). Uneven ice ridges many metres high, and deep cracks that reveal ice-cold seawater are dangers that all Arctic explorers must face. Driving blizzards and thick fog make it difficult to see these hazards, so the going is always slow.

How do explorers stop their ships being crushed by the ice?

Ice floes – enormous chunks of moving ice – are so powerful that they can crush a ship. Polar explorers use ships with reinforced hulls to stop this happening. The *Fram* (left), the ship that took Norwegian Fridtjof Nansen to the North Pole in the 1890s, was one of the first ships of this type.

Who was the first to the North Pole?

American explorer Robert Peary claimed to be the first to reach the North Pole in 1909. He arrived back at his base camp at Cape Columbia, north of Greenland, only two weeks after arriving at the Pole. Many more-recent polar explorers have expressed doubts that he could have travelled that fast and have challenged Peary's claim.

How did Amundsen get to the South Pole first?

Roald Amundsen (below) was the Norwegian explorer who, in 1911, raced British naval officer Robert Falcon Scott to the South Pole. Amundsen won the race and became the first man ever to visit the South Pole. He prepared his expedition carefully, planning every detail and making special advance trips to leave supplies of food along the way. Crucially, he used sledges pulled by dog teams to carry his supplies and so was able to travel more quickly across the ice than his British rivals.

Quick-fire Quiz

1. What are chunks of moving ice called?
a) Flows
b) Floes
c) Flaws

2. Why was Peary's claim questioned?
a) He got back to base so quickly
b) He made no record of his journey
c) He travelled on foot

3. Which animals did Amundsen use for transport?
a) Ponies
b) Dogs
c) Horses

4. What was Edmund Hillary's home country?
a) Britain
b) Australia
c) New Zealand

What happened to Scott's team?

Scott was not as well prepared as Amundsen. He took ponies and a few dogs with him, but the ponies soon died of the cold, and his experience with dogs was limited. Travelling on foot, the food ran low and most of his team had frostbite by the time they found Amundsen's flag at the South Pole. Scott and his men died on the return journey.

Captain Scott

Underworlds

Almost all Earth's surface has been explored. But most of what lies below the surface – in both its caves and oceans – remains a mystery. Only since the 1870s, when ships such as the *Challenger* took to the seas, have we been able to explore the ocean depths.

In about 1840, Augustus Siebe made the first diving suits. A metal helmet with a glass porthole was screwed onto the collar of a flexible waterproof suit (left). The suits were connected by a tube to a surface hand-pump that supplied them with air. So, the divers could not go very deep, but they could stay underwater for as long as they needed.

How deep are ocean trenches?

The deepest trench is the Marianas Trench in the Pacific, which descends almost 11 kilometres below the surface. The *Trieste* (left), a specially built submarine called a bathyscaphe, is the only vessel ever to have gone this deep. Designed by divers Auguste Piccard and his son Jacques to withstand tremendous pressure, it made the dive to the bottom of the Marianas Trench in 1960.

How could you explore underwater without breathing apparatus?

The first underwater swimmers, such as pearl divers (left), could only dive for as long as they could hold their breath. This meant that people could explore only a few metres below the water's surface. Deeper underwater exploration had to be done in a diving bell – a cumbersome tank that could take divers 15 metres below the surface.

What skills do cavers need?

Underground explorers have reached depths of 1.5 kilometres or more in some of the deepest caverns yet discovered. Caves such as the Lamprechtsofen in Austria and the Voronya Cave in Georgia pose great dangers, with their narrow passages, jagged rocks and underground lakes. To explore them, cavers need to develop the skills of mountaineers, sailors and divers.

Who invented the aqualung?

The aqualung was invented in 1943 by French diver Jacques Cousteau (right) and engineer Emile Gagnan. The device consists of a mouthpiece fitted with a special valve connected to an air tank worn on the back. The aqualung transformed shallow-water diving because it left divers free to move about with ease. Using his aqualung, Cousteau made stunning underwater films as he explored the oceans of the world (below).

Quick-fire Quiz

1. Which kind of submersible is the *Trieste*?
a) A bathyscaphe
b) A bathysphere
c) A bathyscan

2. How was air supplied to the first diving suits?
a) With a tank
b) From a hand-pump on the surface
c) From a diving bell

3. Approximately how deep is the Marianas Trench?
a) 1 km
b) 11 km
c) 110 m

4. Which small, remote-controlled robot took pictures of the *Titanic*?
a) *Jason Junior*
b) *Alvin*
c) *Challenger*

How was the wreck of the Titanic filmed?

In 1985, a three-person, titanium-hulled submersible called the *Alvin* (left) was used to investigate the wreck of the *Titanic*, which lay four kilometres below the surface of the Atlantic. The *Alvin* was equipped with a small, remote-controlled robot called *Jason Junior*. This robot was used to explore and film parts of the wreck too small or dangerous for the *Alvin* to reach directly.

Airborne Explorers

To the men and women who first flew aeroplanes, the air was a new world waiting to be conquered. Like their counterparts on land and sea, they had to face danger and hardship. Today, airborne explorers face similar challenges – testing new aircraft or trying to circumnavigate the world by balloon.

Who first crossed the sea in a plane?

The first successful sea crossing in an aeroplane was made by Frenchman Louis Blériot on July 25, 1909. The intrepid aviator flew his *Model XI* aircraft (left) across the English Channel from Les Barraques to Dover. The 39-kilometre flight took him 37 minutes and won him the £1,000 *Daily Mail* prize for crossing the Channel.

Were early flights dangerous?

There was always some danger involved in early flights. Amelia Earhart vanished in 1937 after leaving New Guinea during an attempted round-the-world flight. Another famous aviator, Amy Johnson (below), crashed and disappeared on a routine flight from Scotland to southern England in 1941.

How did Amy Johnson become famous?

British aviator Amy Johnson shot to fame in 1930 when she became the first woman to fly solo from England to Australia in her aircraft, *Jason* (left). During the 19-day, 16,000-kilometre flight, she not only had to cope with terrible weather and jungle runways, but she also had to single-handedly repair her aeroplane after a crash landing.

How are balloons used in exploration?

Vast areas of the sky above our heads are almost impossible for humans to explore – except from specially adapted aircraft. So, scientists send balloons high into the sky – often as far as 42 kilometres into the upper atmosphere (above). All sorts of readings are taken, such as temperature, air pressure and wind speed. These measurements are important for meterologists, who study the atmosphere and weather conditions. This 'remote control' exploration has helped us to learn a lot about our planet.

When is air exploration especially useful?

Deserts, jungles and the icy parts of the globe are all hard to survey and map because of the difficult conditions on the ground. It is far easier to photograph such areas from the air (left). Large parts of Greenland, for example, have been mapped in this way. Aircraft are also used in remote areas to check electric power cables and gas pipelines.

Who was first to fly across the Atlantic Ocean?

In 1927, Charles Lindbergh, an officer in the army air force of the USA, became the first to cross the Atlantic. His aircraft, *Spirit of St Louis* (below), travelled about 5,500 kilometres and the journey took almost 34 hours. During this time, Lindbergh battled rain, fog, heavy cloud, and black ice that formed on the wings, adding to the aircraft's weight and slowing it down.

Quick-fire Quiz

1. Which stretch of water did Louis Blériot cross on July 25, 1909?
   a) The Atlantic
   b) The North Sea
   c) The English Channel

2. What added extra weight to Lindbergh's aircraft?
   a) Extra food
   b) Black ice
   c) Sea birds perching on the wings

3. Who made the first female solo flight from England to Australia?
   a) Amy Johnson
   b) Amelia Earhart
   c) Amelia Johnson

4. Which science uses balloons to gather data?
   a) Biology
   b) Archaeology
   c) Meteorology

Space Exploration

Explorers have travelled all over Earth, but only a few have crossed the 'final frontier' into space. The most dangerous and costly of all forms of exploration, space travel has, in return, given us technological benefits such as satellite communication systems. And it has transformed our knowledge of the Universe.

What does a space suit do?

Made up of as many as 15 layers, the space suit protects the wearer from radiation, low pressure and wildly changing temperatures. The helmet, as well as containing video and communication equipment, also supplies oxygen to the astronaut.

Video camera

Sun visor

15 layers

Layer with circulating fluid to cool or warm the astronaut

Who was the first person in space?

The first person in space was Russian cosmonaut Yuri Gagarin (above). In April 1961, aboard *Vostok 1*, he made a single orbit before parachuting safely back to Earth. This short journey was seen as a challenge by the Americans, and soon the USA and Russia were competing to be the most advanced nation in space.

What is life like on a space station?

Astronauts working on a space station have to adapt to life in weightless conditions, where everything floats around – including people! There is not much space on a space station, so astronauts have to learn how to move about and keep track of their belongings. They eat specially packaged food (left) that does not float all over the place.

Why are space shuttles so useful?

As well as a crew of six astronauts, space shuttles can carry all sorts of different loads into the weightless environment of space. Often, they are used as an economical way to deliver communication and weather satellites into orbit, and they have transported parts of the International Space Station. Shuttles often have Remote Manipulator Systems, 15-metre-long robot arms, which are operated by an astronaut to secure satellites (above) or repair space telescopes.

When was the first moon landing?

The American spacecraft *Apollo 11* made the first Moon landing in July 1969 (right). Astronauts Neil Armstrong and Edwin Aldrin touched down in the lunar module, while Michael Collins circled the Moon in the command module. The two astronauts explored the lunar surface, took samples of rock, carried out experiments and sent live TV pictures back to Earth.

How do you move about in space outside your spacecraft?

When carrying out repairs to their spacecraft, astronauts need to move around freely in space. They use a Manned Manoeuvring Unit (MMU). An MMU is a special backpack that uses rocket thrusters to control direction and movement.

Which craft first landed on Mars?

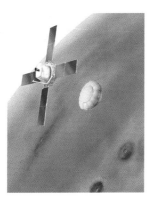

The Russian *Mars 6* reached Mars in 1974, but failed to send back pictures. The first successful landings were the USA's *Viking* probes (left), which touched down in July and September 1976. Both craft took pictures, recorded temperature and wind speed, and analyzed soil samples.

Will people ever live on Mars?

Mars is our nearest neighbour in our solar system, but it has an atmosphere of poisonous carbon dioxide and an average surface temperature of about −23°C, so it would be very difficult for people to live there. One day, astronauts will visit Mars, but they will have to be very well protected at all times (left).

Quick-fire Quiz

1. What is an MMU used for?
a) Eating in space
b) Moving about in space
c) Powering rockets

2. How many of *Apollo 11*'s crew set foot on the moon?
a) One
b) Two
c) Three

3. What was the name of the American probes sent to Mars?
a) *Apollo*
b) *Gemini*
c) *Viking*

4. Which kind of climate does Mars have?
a) Very hot
b) Very cold
c) About the same as Earth

Index

Quick-fire Quiz ANSWERS

Page 5 Ancient Empires
1. c   2. a   3. c   4. b

Page 7 The Mysterious East
1. c   2. b   3. a   4. a

Page 9 Journeys of the Vikings
1. a   2. c   3. b   4. c

Page 11 The Islamic World
1. a   2. b   3. c   4. b

Page 13 Across Asia
1. b   2. a   3. c   4. c

Page 15 The African Coastline
1. a   2. b   3. b   4. c

Page 17 Atlantic Crossings
1. c   2. b   3. a   4. c

Page 19 The Longest Journey
1. a   2. c   3. b   4. a

Page 21 The South Seas
1. c   2. b   3. b   4. b

Page 23 Northern Passages
1. b   2. a   3. c   4. a

Page 25 Exploring N. America
1. b   2. b   3. b   4. c

Page 27 Into Africa
1. c   2. b   3. a   4. c

Page 29 Amazon and Andes
1. c   2. b   3. a   4. c

Page 31 Crossing Australia
1. a   2. b   3. a   4. c

Page 33 World's Coldest Places
1. b   2. a   3. b   4. c

Page 35 Underworlds
1. a   2. b   3. b   4. a

Page 37 Airborne Explorers
1. c   2. b   3. a   4. c

Page 39 Space Exploration
1. b   2. b   3. c   4. b